CALIFORNIA CULTURES SERIES

Filipinos in California

CALIFORNIA CULTURES SERIES

Filipinos in California

Michelle Motoyoshi

Toucan Valley Publications, Inc.

Copyright © 1999 Toucan Valley Publications, Inc.

ISBN 1-884925-92-8

Photographs in this book are used with the permission of the following sources: Special Collections Divison, University of Washington Libraries, Negative No.:UW513 (page 23); Bob Hsiang (page 39); Emil Guillermo (page 45); The World Figure Skating Museum (page 49).

No part of this work may be reproduced in any form, electronic or mechanical, without the written permission of Toucan Valley Publications.

Available from:

Available at-
ARKIPELAGO
The Filipino Bookstore
953 Mission Street
San Francisco, CA 94103
(415)777 0108 Phone
(415)777 0113 Fax
order@arkipelagobooks.com

Toucan Valley Publications, Inc.
PO Box 15520
Fremont CA 94539-2620

www.toucanvalley.com

phone: (800) 236-7946
fax: (888) 391-6943
e-mail: editor@toucanvalley.com

Printed in the United States of America
First Edition

About the *California Cultures Series*

America is a land of diversity. It has been called a melting pot, a salad bowl, a nation of immigrants. Of all the 50 states, California has the most cultural diversity in its population. According to the most recent figures released by the Bureau of the Census, California has 12% of the country's population, yet it has 34% of the Hispanic population and 38% of the Asian population. In 1996, California received 22% of all legal immigration to the United States, according to the California Demographic Research Unit. These immigrants came from Mexico, the Philippines, Vietnam, China, India, El Salvador, Taiwan, and many other countries.

The aim of the *California Cultures Series* is to promote understanding of diversity through the lives of people who live in California.

About the Author

Michelle Motoyoshi received a Ph.D. in sociology from the University of California at Berkeley, where she specialized in race and ethnic relations. She has over eight years of experience conducting research and has been published in academic journals.

Contents

Filipinos in California   9

Carlos Bulosan, *Poet*   23

Philip Vera Cruz, *Labor Leader*   29

Victoria Manalo Draves, *Diver and Olympic Gold Medalist*   35

Robert Kikuchi-Yngojo, *Musician and Performer*   39

Emil Guillermo, *Broadcast Journalist*   45

Tai Babilonia, *Figure Skater*   49

Appendices

   Other Notable Filipino Americans in California   53

   Timeline of the Filipinos in California   55

   Interesting Facts and Figures   57

   For More Information   61

FILIPINOS IN CALIFORNIA

Early Contact with America

The first recorded arrival of Filipinos in America occurred in 1587. While exploring California, the Spanish galleon (large ship) *Nuestra Señora de Esperanza* landed on the central coast. Several Filipinos were on board working as servants. The Filipinos helped the Spaniards scout out the territory. None of them stayed.

Despite that early trip to the American continent, Filipinos would not have significant contact with what would become the United States until 1898. In that year Spain, who had colonized the Philippines over 300 years earlier, surrendered the islands to the United States at the end of the Spanish-American War. The Philippines then became a protectorate of the U.S.; that is, it was put under American control.

When the U.S. took over the Philippines, two significant changes took place. First, Filipinos became U.S. "nationals." This meant they could come to the U.S. whenever they pleased, though they did not have U.S. citizenship. Second, the U.S. introduced American ideas to the Filipinos. The U.S.

set up a school system similar to that in America. In the schools Filipinos learned English and American history and customs. The U.S. also modeled the Filipino government after the American democratic system. They hoped the Filipinos would be loyal to the United States.

Although the Filipinos fought against the American control at first, they later developed an interest in the United States. Many Filipinos came to think of the U.S. as a place of justice and equality where anyone could make their dreams come true. Many decided to come to America in the hopes of making their lives better.

The First Wave of Immigration – 1903-1910

In 1903 the U.S. government established a program for selected students from the Philippines to attend colleges and universities in the U.S. The government provided the Filipino students with scholarships, called *pensions*, to fund their trip to America as well as their college expenses. The students were called *pensionados*.

One of the purposes of the program was to provide Filipinos with advanced training which they could then use to improve their homeland, the Philippines. Upon completing their studies, the pensionados were expected to return to the Philippines to use their knowledge and skills and to spread American values.

The first group of pensionados arrived in California in November of 1903. Most of the men and women who came as pensionados were from wealthy, upper-class families in the Philippines. The majority of them did return to the Philippines when they finished their degrees. The program ended in 1910.

Although the U.S. government stopped funding pensionados, many Filipino students were inspired by their stories of success and decided to immigrate to America themselves. Between 1910 and 1938 about 14,000 Filipino students came and enrolled in American schools, many in California. However, without government sponsorship, these Filipino students found it very difficult to pay all their expenses. They often had to quit school and find a job. They frequently ended up working as laborers and farm workers and rarely made enough money to pay for school. Though some were able to finish their education, many were not.

The Second Wave of Immigration – 1910-1934

At the end of the 19th century, California's farm industry was booming. As a result, the demand for farm laborers increased. This demand attracted immigrants from around the world, especially those who were having trouble finding steady work in their homeland. Filipinos were among the many that came.

Until about 1910, the number of Filipinos coming to California was quite small. But when restrictions on Chinese and Japanese immigration were enacted, a large number of Filipinos came to California to fill the labor shortages. By 1930, there were 30,470 Filipinos in California.

Who Were the Second Wave Immigrants?

The vast majority of Filipinos who came during this immigration were farm workers and other laborers who had little formal education. Most were unmarried men between the ages of 16 to 30. Those men who had wives and families usually left them in the Philippines. Only a very small number of Filipino women immigrated to California during this time.

The Filipinos who came to California lived mostly in the northern and central parts of the state. Some became service workers, taking jobs like janitor, busboy, and bellboy. Most, however, became migrant farm workers, moving to whatever farms had jobs available.

On farms Filipinos were generally hired to do "stoop" labor. That is, they had to plant and pick vegetables that required the worker to remain bent over for long periods of time. The work was physically demanding and often had to be done in very hot weather. At the end of their ten to twelve hour work days, they were exhausted and covered with itchy dust.

Because most of the Filipino workers were men without families, they were often given the worst housing. It wasn't uncommon for almost 100 men to be housed in a single barn. Those same 100 men would have only one faucet and one bathtub between them. There was little comfort and even less privacy.

Fighting for Their Rights

The Filipino farm workers did not accept these poor working conditions quietly. Filipinos were among the first to organize unions and hold strikes. Unions are organized groups of people that try to improve working conditions. Strikes are when workers refuse to do their jobs until their employers (bosses) improve their working conditions.

In 1933 workers in Salinas formed the Filipino Labor Union. The union held a strike in 1934 and demanded higher wages, better working conditions, and recognition of the union. Many local people opposed the union. They burned down the workers' camps, forcing the workers to flee. Though discouraging, the violence didn't keep Filipinos from continuing to fight for their rights.

In 1956 a Filipino farm worker named Larry Dulay Itliong formed the Filipino Farm Labor Union (FFLU), which eventually became the Agricultural Workers Organizing Committee (AWOC). The AWOC was able to obtain some improvements in working conditions for its members, but it didn't gain national attention until it launched a strike against California grape growers.

The strike began in 1965 when Larry and the AWOC convinced 1,000 grape workers to walk out in protest of their poor working conditions. Larry asked César Chávez and his union to join them. They did. What resulted was the largest and most successful farm workers' strike in American history. The two unions eventually merged and became the United Farm Workers union (UFW). The strike ended in 1970 when two of California's largest grape growers signed a contract with the UFW that guaranteed higher pay, benefits, and recognition of the union.

Family and Community

Although working on the farms was difficult, Filipinos were able to create a simple social life for themselves. The Filipinos frequently formed clubs where they could socialize with other Filipinos. They gathered at pool halls and also gambled. Perhaps the most popular pastime, however, was to go to dance halls.

Dance halls became popular because they were one of the few places Filipino men could interact socially with women. Filipino women were a scarcity at the time; for every fourteen Filipino men there was only one Filipino woman.

Because there were so few Filipino women, most Filipino men remained unmarried, but some did find wives of other races. Some married Mexican women. Mexicans and Filipinos shared the Spanish language and the Catholic religion because both their countries had been ruled by Spain. Their common language and religion helped them bond more easily.

Filipino men also dated and occasionally married white women. Most white people in California were unaccustomed to seeing white women with Asian men, and some were opposed to it. Consequently, when a Filipino man was seen with a white woman, the couple was often harassed. To prevent Filipinos and whites from intermarrying, California passed legislation in 1933 that made Filipino-white intermarriage illegal.

Aside from pool halls, dance halls, and the occasional Filipino-owned barber shop, there were few places where Filipinos gathered regularly. They did not develop strong ethnic communities like the Japanese, Chinese, and Koreans did. There were not many Filipino businesses, nor were there long-term settlements that evolved into "Filipinotowns."

One of the reasons "Filipinotowns" did not develop was the Filipinos' colonial history. Because Spain had controlled their country for so long, the Filipinos did not have experience in managing business that could be carried over to the U.S. In addition, most of the Filipinos in California moved around a lot. They intended to return to the Philippines once they had saved some money, rather than establish permanent communities in America.

Discrimination and Prejudice

During this period of immigration, Filipinos in California experienced various forms of prejudice and discrimination. In Watsonville in 1930, 400 white people attacked Filipinos at a dance hall, feeling the

Filipinos were a threat to their jobs and their women. The fighting lasted nearly four days.

Filipinos were refused service in many stores and restaurants owned by white people. They were forced to sit in segregated sections of movie theaters. They were not allowed to own land, and often had trouble renting rooms.

As the number of Filipinos in California grew, so did the prejudice toward them. Because Filipinos were U.S. nationals, the government could not restrict their immigration.

Under pressure from anti-immigration groups, the U.S. government passed the Tydings-McDuffie Act of 1934. The act changed the Philippines from a U.S. protectorate to a commonwealth, which meant the Filipinos were now classified as aliens. The immigration of aliens could be legally restricted, and it was. The number of Filipinos that could come to the U.S. was limited to 50 per year for a ten-year period. By the time the U.S. became involved in World War II, Filipino immigration had ceased completely.

The U.S. Repatriation Act of 1935 offered government-paid transportation back to the Philippines, but very few Filipinos wanted to return.

Filipinos in World War II

Despite suffering from prejudice and discrimination, many Filipinos served in the U.S. Armed Forces in World War II. At first, Filipinos were not allowed to enlist in the armed forces. But they protested. They wanted to defend their homeland, the Philippines, against the Japanese invaders. Finally, President Franklin Roosevelt changed the draft law to include Filipinos.

In California over 16,000 young Filipino men registered for the draft. More than 7,000 recruits served in the First Filipino Infantry Regiment and the Second Filipinos Infantry Regiment. Many of those who served in the armed forces were allowed to become U.S. citizens.

The Filipinos served in the war with great courage and dedication, fighting shoulder to shoulder with other Americans. Their efforts made others view them with greater respect than they had before.

The Third Wave of Immigration – 1965 to Today

When World War II ended, many Filipino war veterans, war brides, and families of servicemen came to California to settle. There was now less prejudice and discrimination against them. The ten-year immigration limit set by the Tydings-McDuffie Act had ended. The Philippines became an independent country. Filipinos in the U.S. could now become naturalized citizens. About 33,000 Filipinos immigrated to the U.S. between 1946 and 1965.

The biggest immigration of Filipinos began after 1965, however. In that year the U.S. government passed the Hart-Celler Act. This act lifted the ban on Asian immigration. This meant that Filipinos were again allowed, in larger but still limited numbers, to come to the United States to settle.

Between 1965 and 1985, approximately 668,870 Filipinos immigrated to the United States. The majority of Filipino immigrants who have come since 1965 are college-educated persons from urban (city) areas. More women than men have immigrated. In 1940 there were about 457 Filipino men for every 100 women. By 1990 there were 86 men for every 100 women.

Most of the Filipino immigrants have settled on the West Coast, primarily in California. In fact, 50 percent of the total Filipino population in the U.S. lives in California. Filipinos are the largest Asian group in the state. Los Angeles is home to the largest Filipino community in the U.S. San Francisco and

San Diego have the third and fourth largest, respectively.

Who Are the Third Wave Immigrants?

Unlike earlier Filipino immigrants, Filipinos from the third wave of immigration have included many professional workers, like doctors, nurses, lawyers, and teachers. They decided to immigrate for several reasons. First, they came because of the political turmoil in the Philippines. Under the rule of Ferdinand Marcos, there was no free speech; the country was under military control; and anyone who openly opposed Marcos would be imprisoned or worse. Many Filipinos were fearful of the Marcos regime and decided to leave the Philippines.

The second and most common reason many Filipinos have immigrated to the United States is greater opportunity for employment (work). A large number of Filipinos are well-educated and professionally trained. But in the Philippines most of the people are quite poor. Few can afford to pay doctors and lawyers and other professionals for their services. In short, there are too many professionals and not enough patients or clients to support them. Consequently, many of these Filipino professionals have come to the U.S. to find employment.

Unfortunately, these Filipino professionals are often unable to work in the positions they were trained for or worked in back home. For example, Filipino doctors must first be licensed to practice medicine in the U.S. But many licensing programs require proof of citizenship or intent to become a citizen. Because of this, many Filipino doctors must take jobs that are lower in pay and status.

Family and Community

Filipino families in California today are much like other American families. Most Filipino American families are not large and do not include as many extended kin as families in the Philippines.

Women in today's Filipino community play an important role in the family. Not only are they in charge of most household matters, they also work to help support the family. Compared to other Asian American groups, Filipino Americans have the highest percentage of women in the workforce.

Though Filipinos work at many types of jobs, there are few Filipino-owned businesses in California. The Filipino community has been more widely dispersed (spread out) than other Asian groups, which has perhaps caused them to be less visible as a whole.

Despite being less visible, Filipinos have still had an impact on California. Slowly but surely they are becoming involved in politics. Though a Filipino has yet to be elected at the state level, some, like Michael Guingona of Daly City, have been elected to city councils. Filipino students at several universities across the state have established Filipino American organizations that have provided support for Filipinos and introduced other Americans to Filipino culture. Through their labor, their expertise, and their perseverance, Filipinos have helped make California what it is today.

CARLOS BULOSAN

Poet

(1913? - 1956)

Carlos Bulosan was one of many Filipinos who immigrated to America in the 1930s. He had to work at menial jobs for little pay, and he faced prejudice and discrimination. But Carlos had his writing. His writing helped him deal with his difficulties, and in time it made him the most famous Filipino American writer in the world.

Carlos was born in Binalonan, Pangasinan, in the Philippines. The year of his birth is either 1913 or 1914. He was a small, frail boy who grew to be only five feet tall.

Carlos grew up in a large family. He had four older brothers and two younger sisters. Being the youngest son, Carlos often had to run errands for his brothers, like getting supplies at the market or fetching water. Carlos didn't mind being told what to do, because his brothers loved and respected him. They taught him to value education and to stick to his beliefs.

Carlos' father, Simeon Bulosan, was a farmer. He owned several acres of land around Binalonan where he grew rice, corn, sugar cane, and vegetables. Autilia Bulosan, Carlos' mother, regularly sold beans and salted fish to add to the family's income. The family was never rich, but during their early years, they were not poor. They had a good house and always had food to eat.

Though they did not have formal schooling, Simeon and Autilia knew education was important. They sent all their children to school, even though it meant they had to sell much of their land. Carlos attended public schools in Binalonan off and on until the age of 13. At that time he attended high school in Lingayen for three years. He dropped out when he found a job in the town of Baguio.

It was in high school that Carlos became more serious about his writing. He worked on the school paper and eventually became the editor. Carlos wrote in English, because English was the main language taught in Filipino schools during that period.

By the time Carlos had dropped out of school, two of his brothers, Aurelio and Dionisio, had already immigrated to California. Both of them had gone with the hope of continuing their education and making their fortune. Carlos wanted to follow them.

In 1930 Carlos got his wish. His parents paid for his trip to the U.S. and gave him a little extra money to help him get settled there. Carlos arrived in Seattle, Washington, on July 22. A few days after his arrival, he took a train to California to join his brother Dionisio, who was living in Lompoc, California.

Carlos soon found that America was not what he had expected. He felt the hostility that some white Americans had toward people of color. He saw how those who weren't white could get only the lowest paying jobs, regardless of their skills or knowledge. Worst of all, he saw how being in America had changed his brother, Dionisio. Once fun-loving, open, and warm, his brother had become anxious and obsessed with money.

After staying a short time with Dionisio, Carlos moved to Los Angeles to live with his other brother, Aurelio. Aurelio had several steady odd jobs and made enough money to support himself and Carlos. Carlos tried to get jobs when he could, but he was often too small and too weak to work for long. Aurelio encouraged Carlos to focus on his writing. Carlos heeded his brother's advice. He spent many days reading books and writing at the Los Angeles Public Library.

Carlos worked very hard at his writing, but when he first started sending his work to magazines, he received rejection after rejection. Still, he kept at it. Finally in 1932, some of his poems were published in a book called *California Poets: An Anthology of 244 Contemporaries*. But Carlos wanted to do more than publish a few poems, so he started his own literary magazine in 1934.

Called *The New Tide*, the magazine featured articles, short stories, and poetry by well-known writers like William Carlos Williams. Aurelio and some of Carlos' friends provided money for the magazine and also labor. They worked as the staff. Unfortunately, Carlos had to stop publishing the magazine after only two issues, due to a lack of funds.

Carlos didn't let the closing of his magazine discourage him. He continued to write and to send his work to publishers. Carlos also spent time visiting other Filipinos around the West. He became active in the labor movement.

During this time Carlos began to realize that he could use his writing to help improve the situation of Filipinos. Through his writing, he could describe and explore the Filipino American experience. He could shed light on their personal struggles in adjusting to a new and sometimes hostile country. He could be a voice for Filipinos in America.

It would be a few years before Carlos would fulfill his mission. In 1936 he came down with tuberculosis, a contagious disease which affects the lungs. Carlos spent two years in the hospital. When he was well enough to go home, he picked up his life where he had left it, but the illness had weakened him.

About four years after his bout with tuberculosis, Carlos finally began to receive recognition for his writing. Two volumes of his poetry, *Letter from America* and *Chorus for America*, were published in 1942. That same year, Carlos began working on *America Is in the Heart*, which would become his most famous work. In 1943, *The Voice of Bataan*, a collection of poems about the soldiers who fought in the Battle of Bataan in World War II, was published and received favorable reviews.

America Is in the Heart was published in 1946. The book tells the story of Filipinos in California. The central character is modeled after Carlos himself, and many of the incidents in the book are loosely based on things he himself experienced. For this reason, many people have thought *America Is in the Heart* is an autobiography, but it is not. It is not only Carlos' story, it is the story of many Filipinos who lived and struggled in California.

After the publication of *America Is in the Heart*, Carlos divided his time between writing, working with the farm labor movement in California and Washington, and travelling across the country giving lectures. Through all of his activities, Carlos worked tirelessly to educate people about Filipinos in America and to combat racism against them.

Carlos Bulosan died in 1956 from lung congestion, a complication of his previous tuberculosis. His contribution to Filipinos in California and around the world continues. On December 11, 1983, Carlos' hometown of Binalonan erected a monument in his honor and named a street after him. More importantly, *America Is in the Heart* has become a primary text in many introductory Asian American Studies classes. Carlos would probably be pleased to know his writing continues his life's work – educating others about Filipino Americans.

PHILIP VERA CRUZ

Labor Leader

(1904 - 1989)

Like many other Asian immigrants, Philip Vera Cruz encountered racism and inequality when he came to America. Rather than accepting these unjust circumstances, Philip decided to fight for change. He became an important leader in the struggle for better pay and working conditions in the California farm industry.

On Christmas Day, 1904, Philip Vera Cruz was born to Andriano Vera Cruz and Maria Villamin in a small town called Saong in the northern Philippine province of Ilocos Sur. He was the oldest of three children. His sister Leonor and his brother Martin were both more than 15 years younger than Philip. They were still very young children when he made his trip to America.

Philip's parents were peasant farmers who relied on their land to survive. They had no formal education, but were able to read and write a little. Generous and kind, they did what they could to help their children and those who needed help in their village.

Philip's father was a rather frail man who needed help farming his land. He wanted Philip to stay on the farm, but Philip had other ideas. Philip wanted to go to school. Under Spanish rule, Filipinos had been denied the opportunity to get an education. When the Americans took over, education was made available to anyone who could afford it. Recognizing the value in education, Philip asked his father if he could attend, but his father forbade it. Philip went anyway, without telling his parents.

It wasn't long before Philip's parents found out from a relative that Philip was attending school. Though surprised, his parents accepted it. They knew Philip was independent and determined, so they let him pursue his goal. In fact, as Philip needed money to purchase books, paper, and other supplies, his parents sold portions of their land to help pay his expenses.

In 1926 Philip immigrated to the U.S. His father sold the last piece of land he owned to pay for Philip's passage to America. His father told him, "There's nothing left for your brother and sister now. You take it (the money) because you need it. Use it, but don't forget that you've got to help them later, too." Philip took the words to heart. Throughout the rest of his life, Philip sent thousands of dollars back to his brother and sister, even when he had little money to spare, so they could obtain an education and get good jobs.

When Philip came to America he intended, as many Filipinos did, to work, save some money, and return to the Philippines better off than when he had left. As with many Filipinos, things didn't work out the way Philip had planned.

During the 1920s and 30s, the only jobs available to Filipino immigrants were manual labor jobs, like busboy or farm worker. Having worked on farms before, Philip went to the fields. He got jobs picking vegetables, which involved extremely difficult labor. He had to remain bent over in the hot sun for nine or ten hours a day, earning 70 cents, then eventually 80 cents per hour. Philip had to move frequently to find work, and though he worked consistently, the low pay he received kept him from saving large amounts of money.

In addition to the long, hard work days, Philip also had to deal with prejudice and discrimination. Wherever he went in pursuit of work, he encountered segregation. He wasn't allowed to sit in certain parts of movie theaters or to eat in certain restaurants because he wasn't white. Many white people looked upon him as if he were inferior. It sometimes upset Philip, even though he knew he was as good a person as they were.

As Philip moved from job to job, he saw that farm workers, regardless of their ethnic background, were not treated with the respect they deserved. Growers took advantage of them all. Philip soon decided that he wanted to do something about the terrible situation of farm workers. He became involved in labor organizing.

Labor organizing involved educating workers about their unfair work situation and helping them form unions (organized groups that try to improve working conditions). Unions may organize strikes (when workers refuse to do their jobs until their employers improve the working conditions) or boycotts (when people refuse to buy a certain product until the employers treat their workers better).

Philip moved to Delano, California, in 1943. While he worked in the vineyards there, he participated in many labor organizing activities. For example, he joined in the Stockton asparagus strike of 1948. In the late 1950's he served as leader of the short-lived National Farm Labor Union (NFLU), and in the 1960s, he joined the Agricultural Workers' Organizing Committee (AWOC).

Around the time Philip joined AWOC, he learned that his mother was seriously ill. Because he was so heavily involved in the union, Philip had little time and even less money. He couldn't afford to go to the Philippines to visit his mother. She died in 1972. Philip had not seen her since he left the Philippines 46 years earlier.

Despite the emotional and financial sacrifices he had to make, Philip stuck with the union and did what he could to make it a success. One of the most important things he did was help launch the Delano strike against grape growers. Once AWOC had started the strike, Philip and other AWOC leaders convinced César Chávez and his union to join. The Delano grape strike was the biggest and most successful farm labor strike in U.S. history.

As the two unions worked together, they eventually decided to merge and form a single union. That union became known as the United Farm Workers (UFW). At the UFW's 1971 national convention, Philip was elected second vice-president. He was the highest ranking Filipino official in the union. His position was second only to Dolores Huerta and César Chávez.

Although he still believed in the necessity of the UFW, over the years Philip became increasingly unhappy with the development of the union. He felt that the leadership of the UFW was largely neglecting the needs of the Filipino workers. Philip tried hard to get the UFW to meet the needs of its Filipino membership, but often he was alone against the opposition. Frustrated, Philip finally left the UFW in 1977.

Even though he left the union, Philip continued to speak out against injustice here in America as well as in the Philippines. In 1987 he was awarded the Ninoy M. Aquino Award in recognition of his lifelong service to Filipinos in America. Philip Vera Cruz died in Bakersfield, California, at the age of 89.

VICTORIA MANALO DRAVES

Diver and Olympic Gold Medalist

(1924 -)

The daughter of a Filipino father and an English mother, Victoria Manalo Draves was a national champion diver who became the first woman to win an Olympic gold medal in both the 10-meter platform and 3-meter springboard diving competitions.

Born December 31, 1924, in San Francisco, California, Victoria became interested in diving in high school. She would often practice at the Fairmont Hotel or at the Crystal Bath Plunge. Both places had public swimming pools with diving boards.

Victoria graduated from high school in 1938. She then attended college in San Francisco, but she dropped out when World War II broke out. She decided to start competing in amateur diving competitions.

Because of the prejudice against Filipinos at the time, Victoria used her mother's maiden name, Taylor, as her last name when she was in competitions. If the officials knew she was part Filipino, they might not let her compete.

In 1941 Jack Lavery, a coach from the Fairmont Swim Club, noticed how well Victoria could dive. He told Sammy Lee, a national champion diver, about Victoria.

Two years later, Sammy Lee watched Victoria dive. He was amazed at her natural diving abilities. She was able to do things, like straighten her back before entering the water, that usually took divers a great deal of coaching to master. After being introduced to Victoria, Sammy told her that she would be a diving champion. From that point on, Sammy Lee became a mentor to Victoria.

Victoria competed in her first national diving competition in Shakemack, Indiana, in 1944. Despite fierce competition, she placed in the top four in both the 3-meter springboard and the 10-meter platform diving events. A year later, she competed in the nationals again and placed in the top four.

Sammy Lee felt Victoria could do better. He advised her to get a new coach, one that could help her compete at a higher level. He suggested she ask Lyle

Draves, a coach at the Athen's Swim Club in Oakland, California, if he would train her.

Later that year, Victoria started training with Lyle Draves. She also fell in love with him. The two were married in 1946. At the national championships that same year, Victoria won the 10-meter platform diving competition. It was her first national championship. It was also the first time she had beat her arch rival, Zoen Olsen.

In 1948 Victoria tried out for the U.S. Olympic diving team. She barely qualified for the team. Her rival, Zoen, had come out ahead of her.

At a dinner just prior to their Olympic diving competition, Zoen claimed that she was going to win both diving events. Victoria took Zoen's claim as a challenge and put her all into her diving. Victoria won the gold medal in both the 10-meter platform and 3-meter springboard events. She was the first woman to do so in the same Olympics.

When Victoria returned home from the 1948 Olympics, she was considered a hero. She performed in exhibitions around the country. For a time, there was even talk of having her star in movies. In 1949 she was honored in the Philippines.

Not long after the Olympics, Victoria dropped out of diving competition and started a family with her husband, Lyle. They had four children. Because of her diving accomplishments, Victoria has been inducted into the International Swimming Hall of Fame in Fort Lauderdale, Florida.

ROBERT KIKUCHI-YNGOJO

Musician and Performer

(1953 -)

As a pre-med student at the University of California at Davis, Robert Kikuchi-Yngojo may not have imagined himself performing for people around the world, but that is precisely what he does. By following his heart, Robert has become a successful musician and theater performer who is one of the pioneers of the California Filipino and Asian American music scene.

Robert was born September 22, 1953, in San Francisco, California. His mother, Delores Yngojo, immigrated from the Philippines to the U.S. when she was four years old. His Japanese-American father, John Kikuchi, was born in Vallejo, California, in 1917. John and Delores had five children, four sons and one daughter. Robert was the third born.

When Robert was a toddler, his parents moved to Concord, California, a suburb located east of San

Francisco. Though it was a predominantly white neighborhood, Concord had a small community of Japanese Americans, and neighboring Pittsburgh had a growing Filipino American community. Robert and his family spent time with both groups, making friends and learning about both cultures. Robert went to Japanese language school and regularly participated in his mother's Filipino dance troupe. In the dance troupe, he wore a *barong tagalog* shirt, a traditional Filipino garment made of nipa palm fiber. He also listened to Filipino music.

Although Robert spent much of his time in the Filipino and Japanese communities, he also interacted with the larger white community in which he lived. Robert learned how to get along with everyone. However, he felt most white people didn't accept him. Sometimes he was teased or bullied because he looked different from the other children. Some of them would pull their eyes into slits and make fun of Robert's Asian eyes. Experiences like these made Robert feel bad, but he didn't let them keep him down. In fact, later in his life, he sometimes used his experiences in his performances.

After graduating from Clayton Valley High School in 1971, Robert attended the University of California at Davis. At that time, he was planning on becoming a medical doctor. He majored in pre-med and zoology, hoping to be accepted to a medical school.

To help prepare himself for medical school, Robert became involved in the Asian Health Concern. This organization provided free medical services to Filipino farm laborers in the San Joaquin Valley. Through the organization, Robert met *Manongs*, older generation Filipino farm workers. He saw first-hand the effects racism, poverty and hard labor had on the Manongs. The experience moved him deeply. He wrote a song to express his feelings and called it "To the Manongs of Walnut Grove."

The song became popular among student groups at colleges across the state. In fact, the song became so popular Robert was asked to perform it at political rallies and other gatherings. He enjoyed performing and being a part of political and cultural events, but he continued preparing to be a doctor.

By the time Robert graduated from U.C. Davis in 1976, he had learned that he was not accepted to medical school. Discouraged, Robert turned to his music to help him deal with his disappointment. Soon he remembered how much he loved to sing and perform. More importantly, he began to realize that singing and performing is what he really wanted to do.

In addition to his music, Robert was also interested in the political issues of the times. Growing up in the 1960s and 1970s, Robert witnessed the Civil Rights Movement and the Vietnam War protests. These events had a profound influence on Robert. They made him realize that he wasn't the only one who had experienced prejudice. These events also helped convince him that people can change unjust circumstances if they believe in themselves and stand up for their rights.

Slowly but surely, Robert began to combine his love for music and performing with his passion for social justice. He became involved with several Filipino political and social groups, helping them write and perform theater pieces. While working with one of these political organizations, Robert was given the opportunity to write and perform music for a play about the people of Mindanao, a southern island of the Philippines. Through doing the music for the play, Robert was introduced to Kulintang gongs, a percussion instrument from Mindanao.

Robert enjoyed playing the Kulintang gongs, but he knew he needed to learn more about them. While on tour in Seattle, Robert met Vasopay Cadar, Ric Trimillos and Danny Kalanduyan, three masters of the Kulintang gongs. They trained him to play the gongs in traditional Filipino fashion. Robert wanted to further his training, so in 1981 he went to the Philippines to study for several months.

When he had finished his training in the Philippines, Robert was very excited about the new knowledge he had gained about Filipino music. He wanted to share it with people back in San Francisco. Robert received a grant from the California Arts Council to help him start Kulintang gong classes. From the classes a performance group emerged called the San Francisco Kulintang Ensemble, which was later renamed Kalilang (meaning to celebrate).

Between the classes and the performance group, Robert had laid the foundation for the development of Filipino ethnic music and dance in Northern California.

In 1981 Robert married Nancy Wang (pronounced Wong), a Chinese American choreographer (person who plans and designs dance performances). Nancy shares Robert's passion for ethnic music and theater. Nancy and Robert have two children, a son named Zachary and a daughter named Xiani.

When Robert was involved with Kalilang, he also played with an ethnic jazz fusion band called the Noh Buddies. With this group, Robert began to see the potential in combining different kinds of Asian and Western music. Along with his wife Nancy, Robert formed Eth-Noh-Tec, a theater duo that uses music, dance, and storytelling to educate people about other cultures, racism, and identity.

In Eth-Noh-Tec Robert has achieved his primary career goal -- to combine his music and theater talents with his desire to address contemporary issues. Today Eth-Noh-Tec travels around the world, using their performances to teach people of all ages and ethnicities about diversity and the possibility of peace. By sharing his passion and pride in his culture, Robert helps others appreciate not only other cultures, but also themselves.

EMIL GUILLERMO

Broadcast Journalist

(1955 -   )

Listening to the radio at night when he was young, Emil Guillermo dreamed of having a career in radio. Through hard work and perseverance, Emil made his dream come true. He became one of the first Filipino Americans to have a successful career in broadcast journalism.

Born October 9, 1955, Emil was raised in San Francisco. His parents were both immigrants from the Philippines. His father, Emiliano, worked as a fry cook, while his mother, Josefa, took care of Emil and his sister. The family didn't have much money, and they moved around the city frequently to find low-cost housing. But that didn't steal all the adventure from his childhood.

Growing up, Emil was allowed to be independent. He did many things on his own, like going by bus to the Oakland Athletics' baseball games. One of his favorite things to do, though, was spend time in nearby Dolores Park. There he would play on youth league teams in soccer, baseball, and football. In between seasons, he liked to spend time with his friends.

Emil applied himself to his studies and did very well in school. At Everett Junior High he got straight A's. He continued to earn good grades when he attended Lowell High School, one of the most competitive and well-respected high schools in California. In fact, Emil's school achievements were good enough to get him a scholarship to Harvard University.

At Harvard Emil majored in history, but his interests lay in writing and the media. He worked as a disc jockey at the university's radio station as well as for the *Harvard Lampoon*, a noted humor magazine. In 1975, before starting his junior year, Emil decided he wanted to try working in radio professionally. He landed a job at a Houston radio station. During his one and a half years in Houston, Emil built up a large audience. Although he enjoyed working there, he decided to return to Harvard and complete his degree. He did so in 1977, after only three years of study.

After graduating, Emil decided to pursue television news broadcasting. He got his first on-air reporting job in 1979 at station KOLO in Reno, Nevada. In addition to reporting, he also worked as a sportscaster and back-up anchor. After about a year in Reno, Emil took a job in Dallas at station KXAS. Fourteen months later, he was offered a position at KRON in San Francisco. Emil was a reporter at KRON for about seven years and covered a variety of news stories.

While working as a reporter, Emil learned that there was more to broadcast journalism than simply reporting facts on current events. There was also a need for opinion pieces and social commentary. Emil became very interested in that aspect of broadcasting. After working at KRON, Emil started his own radio show, called "Bay Area Filipino with Emil Guillermo." The show featured news and entertainment stories, as well as personal essays by Emil. Though the show was successful, Emil decided to leave it when he was offered a position with National Public Radio (NPR) in 1989.

At NPR Emil became the weekend anchor of the popular news show "All Things Considered." He was the first Asian American to anchor a national radio news show. He was also the first Asian American male to anchor any national news program, on radio or television. On the show, Emil got to do what he does best: report on current affairs and give his views on political issues.

In 1991 Emil left NPR and began hosting his own radio show in Washington, D.C. Being in the nation's capitol increased Emil's interest in politics. He decided he wanted to see the political process close up, so in 1993 he became press secretary and speechwriter for Norm Mineta, one of California's representatives in the U.S. Congress. Through his job, Emil learned things about American politics and government that most people never hear about. But perhaps the most important thing he learned was that he missed being in the media.

Emil returned to San Francisco and resumed his career as a writer and broadcaster. Today he continues to write articles for a variety of magazines like *Asian Week* and *Filipinas*. He has published a collection of essays called *Amok: Essays from an Asian American Perspective*.

Emil has also co-created a television news show called *New California Media*. In this show, as in all his work, Emil tries to give voice to communities and people that are too often ignored by mainstream news shows. He remains committed to this mission and to redefining what it means to be an American in an era of ethnic diversity.

TAI BABILONIA

Figure Skater

(1960 -   )

At first, Tai Bailonia didn't want to ice skate with Randy Gardner. She didn't want to hold his hand. But her coach, Mabel Fairbanks, told her to do it. When she did, the two found they skated very well together, so well, in fact, they eventually became one of the most successful pair-skaters in U.S. history.

Tai Babilonia was born September 22, 1960, in Mission Hill, California. Her father, a Filipino American, worked as a detective in the Los Angeles Police Department. Her mother, a Caucasian (white) American, was a housewife.

Tai began skating at the age of seven when her Japanese godfather took her to a birthday party at a skating rink. She fell in love with the sport immediately. Though Tai began as a singles skater, her coach, Mabel, believed Tai and Randy could become world champion pairs-skaters. After some persistent persuading, Mabel got the two youngsters to begin skating together.

To become champion skaters, Tai and Randy had to practice skating four to six hours a day. But they still had to go to school and do their homework. On top of that, they also managed to fit in jazz dance and ballet lessons, as well as physical fitness exercises, like weight lifting. It was a grueling schedule, which they kept for about ten years.

About four years after being paired together, Tai and Randy won the 1973 National Junior pairs skating title. Only a year later, they skated in the U.S. National Championships and placed second, which won them the opportunity to compete in the World Championships. At age 13 and 15, respectively, Tai and Randy were the youngest pair in U.S. history to qualify for the U.S. World team.

Although Tai and Randy only placed tenth in their first World Championships, the two went on to win the U.S. National pairs competition five straight years in a row. Along the way, they intensified their training routine, adding more resistance exercises and jogging to increase their stamina. In 1979 their rigorous training finally paid off. They won the

World Championships. They were the first American skating pair to do so in 29 years.

Having won the World Championship, Tai and Randy were eager to compete in the 1980 Olympics. They were favored to win and were very excited about the prospect of winning a medal. But tragedy struck the pair only two weeks before the Olympic competition. Randy seriously injured his leg.

At first the pain from his injury went away, so Randy didn't tell Tai about it. But while practicing before their competition, Randy re-injured his leg. He couldn't do even simple jumps. Bitterly disappointed, Tai and Randy had to pull out of the Olympics.

Tai was very upset about missing the Olympics, but she and Randy never talked about how they felt. Tai kept all her feelings inside and didn't share them with anyone. After taking a short break from skating, Tai and Randy became professional skaters and started touring with the Ice Capades.

Working with the Ice Capades was very difficult for Tai. Because she was on the road all the time, she didn't have time to make close friends, and she wasn't able to see her family very often. Tai felt homesick and very lonely. To try to make herself feel better, Tai started to drink alcohol. It only made her feel worse. She felt even more alone and started to feel physically ill. And though she didn't realize it at the time, she was endangering other people, especially her partner Randy, when she would skate or drive while she was under the influence of alcohol.

In 1988 Tai decided to quit skating. She was so depressed she hid in her house and hardly talked to anyone. At last, she reached out to her family and got help. She went to Alcoholics Anonymous and saw a counselor regularly. Her family stuck by her, as did her friend Randy. Tai finally started to feel happy and healthy again.

In 1996 Tai went back to skating and performed with Randy. Though she and Randy don't always get high scores like they did in the past, Tai enjoys skating more than ever. Having faced the unhappiness inside her, she has become a stronger person who can now skate out of love for the sport.

OTHER NOTABLE FILIPINO AMERICANS IN CALIFORNIA

Bobby Balceda
Born in San Pedro, California, he was the first Filipino to become a Major League Baseball player. He played for the Cincinnati Reds in 1956.

Tia Carrere
An actress and singer, she has been in several movies, including *Wayne's World* and *True Lies*.

Maryles Casto
The founder, owner, and manager of Casto Travel, the largest privately owned corporate travel agency in northern California, she was appointed to the California council to promote business ownership by women.

Jocelyn Enriquez
Born and raised in San Francisco, she is a singer who is one of the first Filipino Americans to break into the American popular music industry.

Michael Guingona
In 1993 he was the first Filipino American elected to the city council of Daly City.

Sumi Sevilla Haru
An actor, producer, and journalist, she has served as the president of the Screen Actors Guild and has fought for greater representation of minorities in the television and film industry.

Larry Dulay Itliong
A labor leader, he formed the Agricultural Workers Organizing Committee (AWOC) with Philip Vera Cruz and helped to launch the successful Delano grape strike in 1965.

Danny Modelo
Raised in San Diego, he is the first Filipino American animal trainer at Sea World.

Marion Lacadia Obera
Appointed to the Los Angeles judicial bench in 1970, she was the first Filipino American to serve as a judge in the continental United States.

Mañuel Ocampo
One of the most celebrated Filipino American contemporary artists, his paintings have been displayed in exhibits around the world.

Ramon Sison
A medical doctor and an actor, he was appointed to the Medical Quality Review Committee of the California State Board of Medical Examiners.

TIMELINE OF THE FILIPINOS IN CALIFORNIA

1587 The Spanish galleon *Nuestra Señora de Esperanza* lands in California on October 18. Filipino members of the crew serve as scouts.

1898 The United States acquires the Philippines.

1903 The *pensionado* program begins. In November about 100 Filipinos arrive in California to attend universities.

1921 The first Filipino newspaper in the continental United States, *The Philippine Independent News,* begins publication in Salinas, California.

1933 The Filipino Labor Union (FLU) is established to help Filipino farm workers obtain better working conditions.

1934 Tydings-McDuffie Act is enacted. The act makes the Philippines a commonwealth and promises the islands independence in ten years. The main purpose of the act is to prevent further immigration of Filipinos to the U.S.

1935 The Repatriation Act of 1935 is enacted. The act provides funds to help Filipinos return home. Only 2,190 Filipinos relocate.

1942 Filipinos are drafted to serve in World War II. Over 7,000 recruits serve in the First Filipino Infantry Regiment and in the Second Filipino Infantry Regiment.

1965 Agricultural Workers' Organizing Committee (AWOC) begins the strike against California's grape growers, a strike that would later become associated with César Chávez and the UFW.

1965 Immigration Act of 1965, also known as the Hart-Celler Act, is passed, lifting previous restrictions on immigration from Asian countries, including the Philippines.

1970 Marion Lacadia Obera is appointed as a judge in Los Angeles, becoming the first Filipino American to hold such a position.

1973 The first Filipino American commercial bank in the U.S. opens in Los Angeles, California. Called the International Bank of California, it is the first bank to include Filipinos in its management.

INTERESTING FACTS AND FIGURES

Filipino American population over the years:

Year	United States	California
1910	2,767	5
1920	26,634	2,674
1930	108,260	30,470
1940	98,535	31,408
1950	122,707	40,424
1960	181,614	67,134
1970	336,731	135,248
1980	774,652	358,378
1990	1,406,770	733,941

In 1990:

California had 12% of the U.S. population and about 50% of the Filipino American population.

Filipino Americans are the largest Asian ethnic group in California. They are the second largest in the nation.

Filipino Americans made up about 2.5% of California's population.

Foods from the Philippines

Chicken and Pork Adobo – Considered the Philippines national dish, the chicken and/or pork is stewed in a sauce of vinegar, soy sauce, garlic and bay leaves.

Empanada – A flaky turnover filled with beef or chicken.

Halo-Halo – A milkshake made from about ten ingredients including jackfruit, sweet red beans, coconut, egg custard, red gelatin, and milk.

Leche Flan – A popular dessert, it is an egg custard topped with a sweet syrup.

Lechon – Whole roast pig, usually cooked for special occasions.

Lumpia – Fried egg rolls filled with pork and vegetables. They are usually served with a vinegar and garlic sauce.

Pancit – Stir-fried noodles with chopped fresh vegetables and thinly-sliced sausage and tiny shrimp.

Ube – Purple taro root used to flavor ice cream and other desserts.

Words from the Philippines

Boondocks (boonies) – From the Tagalog word "bundok" (meaning mountain), U.S. soldiers borrowed the word to describe the jungle areas where they fought in the Philippines. Boondocks, or its shortened version "boonies," now refers to any undeveloped backcountry area.

Pinoy or Pinay – Another term for "Filipino," especially one living abroad, the word was invented by mainland Americans to refer to Filipinos in a negative way. Recently, the word has been reclaimed by the Filipino community and is no longer considered negative. "Pinay" (pronounced pee-neye) refers only to women Filipinos, while "Pinoy" refers to male, or male and female, Filipinos.

Manong – An Ilocano (a northern Filipino language) term used when addressing elders to show them respect. In the U.S. it has become associated with the first generation of labor migrants that came in the 1920s and 30s.

Popular Filipino Holidays

Christmas – The most important and widely celebrated holiday among Filipinos. In the Philippines Christmas activities typically begin December 16 and continue through January 6. In the U.S. the time of celebration is usually shorter. Common Filipino Christmas traditions are hanging *parol* (paper lanterns in the shape of stars), attending midnight mass on Christmas Eve, and having a huge feast which includes *lechon* (roast pig), *bibingka* (rice cakes baked in clay ovens), and *puto bumbong* (rice steamed in bamboo tubes topped with fresh coconut and sugar).

Philippine Independence Day – Celebrated June 16, it is the day Filipinos commemorate winning their independence from Spain in 1898.

Other things from Filipino Culture

Yo-Yo – In the 1500s Filipino hunters created a yo-yo made of large, circular wood disks and sturdy twine. The yo-yo was thrown at the feet of an animal, ensnaring its legs. In the 1920s an American named Donald Duncan saw the yo-yo in action. He decided to turn it into a toy by making a smaller version of it. He kept the Tagalog name.